*Too Much of a Good Thing*

# Too Much of a Good Thing

## John Sparrow

The University of Chicago Press
Chicago and London

JOHN SPARROW was a practicing lawyer in London
before he became Warden of All Souls College, Oxford.
He is the author of several books, among them
*After the Assassination, Mark Pattison
and the Idea of a University,* and *Visible Words.*

The University of Chicago Press, Chicago 60637
The University of Chicago Press, Ltd., London
© 1977 by The University of Chicago
All rights reserved. Published 1977
Printed in the United States of America

*Library of Congress Cataloging in Publication Data*

Sparrow, John Hanbury Angus, 1906-
    Too much of a good thing.

    (Sara Halle Schaffner lecture series; 1976)
    1. Social problems—Addresses, essays, lectures.
2. Equality—Addresses, essays, lectures.   3. Individuality—Addresses, essays, lectures.   4. Criminal
justice, Administration of.   I. Title.   II. Series.
HN18.S74         309         77-6389
ISBN 0-226-76848-1

# Contents

# Preface

The contents of this little book are the fruits of an invitation from the Committee on Social Thought of the University of Chicago, who asked me to deliver the Sara Halle Schaffner Lectures at the University in 1976. When extending their invitation, the Committee gave me a wide discretion as to the topics I might take for my lectures, stipulating only that my theme should be one that lay within the field indicated by the title Social Thought.

This presented me with a problem: how should I interpret "Social Thought"? I took it to mean reflections about society, about the world in which we live together, and I imagined that I had been asked, "What do you think about the way the world is going? What do you see as being the most significant, the most important, tendencies of the age? What do you feel about them?" My answers to these questions consisted, as the following pages will show, simply of my own reflections. I am not a philosopher, nor a sociologist, nor a politician; I have no theory to expound, no principles to enunciate, no cause to advocate: all I have to offer is my personal impressions, my personal reactions. I have tried to analyze them and to sort them out, but they remain essentially personal, my own account of what seem to me to be the most significant tendencies of the age.

What do I mean by "the age"? I mean the period, just over a human generation, that has elapsed since the end of the Second World War. I cannot help contrasting the old days with today; "the old days" for me means "before the War"; "today" means "since the War." This isn't just a convenient chronological division, like the turn of a century; the War didn't only divide the pre-War from the post-War world; it helped to change the pre-War into the post-War world. Each of the succeeding decades, the fifties, the sixties, the seventies, may have contributed distinguishable waves, perhaps even cross-currents, of its own; but over the whole period a new tide, I think, has set in.

I must place "the age" in space as well as time, for when one speaks of "the tendencies of the age," one must be thinking of a particular society, or particular societies, in which the tendencies manifest themselves. The suggestions I have to offer are based on my own observation of what is happening in my own country, and on what, so far as I can judge, is happening in other countries in Western Europe. I offer no judgment in regard to the United States.

What then are the significant tendencies that have shown themselves in Great Britain since the end of the Second World War? I think they are tendencies towards increased liberty, increased equality, and increased humanity. As my main title indicates, I think that all these tendencies are good things, but that it is possible for them to go too far. In the chapters that follow, I try to explain what I mean by "going too far" in regard to each of them.

I cannot conclude this preface without expressing my gratitude to the University of Chicago for the hospitality extended to me as Schaffner Lecturer and for the indulgent reception that was given to my lectures.

# Equality

Equality, Humanity, Liberty—it sounds like the French Revolution! But the tendencies towards increased equality, increased humanity, increased liberty, that I observe making themselves felt, at any rate in my own country, do not operate, or so it seems to me, in a political or an economic context. If you compare Britain today with Britain as it was in the 1920s and the 1930s, you have to conclude that by and large in the political and economic fields the battle for liberty and equality has been won. When I was a boy, organized labor was practically unrepresented in Parliament. There was a rudimentary Labour Party, with less, I think, than a dozen seats in the House of Commons. Power was shared between the Conservatives and the Liberals, both of which parties consisted almost entirely of members who were drawn from, and represented, the governing class. After the First World War, things changed quickly: the first Labour government in England took office in 1924, the year before my freshman's year at Oxford. Since the Second World War, the Liberal Party has almost disappeared, and power has been shared between Labour and Conservatives. Labour has always been the party of the Left, the majority of the working class, with a strong infusion of intellectuals; the Conservatives have been the party of the Right, the propertied and the professional classes, with an infusion of the aristocracy and the support of about a quarter of the working class. But today there is less to distinguish the Labour Party from the Conservatives, whether in their composition or in their policies, than there was to distinguish the Liberals from the Conservatives in the old days. There is no longer a governing class: those who in effect govern the country are no longer identifiable with any social stratum. The most obvious difference in policy between the political parties, a cynic might say, is that the Labour Party offers higher bribes to the Trade Unions than do the Conservatives.

As for economic equality, there are still rich and poor today in Great Britain, though not so many very rich as in the pre-War world, and far fewer very poor. The gap between the two is being perpetually reduced by increasingly heavy taxation on the one hand, and ever-rising wages and a lavish provision of "Public Welfare" on the other.

Finally, social equality. Britain is still, I suppose, a class-ridden society compared with the United States.[1] I can only say that compared with the

1. "The lower classes" is a phrase no longer in use; but anomalously) "the middle classes" and even the adjective "upper-class" (whence the colloquial "U" and "non-U") are still current; and the word "gentleman" retains a social connotation that is well understood, if difficult to explain.

Britain of the old days, society in Britain today is practically classless. You may recall Matthew Arnold's essay on Equality, published almost exactly a hundred years ago, in his *Mixed Essays* (1879). In that essay Arnold, taking for his text the maxim "Choose Equality," contrasts the English love of inequality with the passion for equality that has always characterized the French. France, he declared, was the most civilized of nations, and it was to her passion for equality that she owed that pre-eminence. England, compared with France, was uncivilized, and that was because English society was rigidly stratified in three social orders, which he called "our eternal trio"—the Barbarians (the aristocracy), the Philistines (the middle class), and the Populace. England, in Arnold's view, would never become a truly civilized country until that hierarchy was abolished. The best and quickest way to abolish it, he thought, was to reform the law of inheritance in conformity with the Continental model, so that great landed estates, or large accumulations of property, should be broken up and redistributed with each succeeding generation.

It wasn't until after Arnold's death that the first step was taken. The Finance Act of 1894 introduced Estate Duty, a levy on inheritance which almost revolutionized the existing system of taxation. When an estate changed ownership on a death, a fraction of it, calculated at a rate determined by its total value, was to be confiscated by the State. The effect of Death Duties, which have now reached crippling proportions, of ever-rising taxes on income, and of vast increases in wages and in expenditure on Public Welfare and on State education—to which causes one must add the leveling and unifying influence of the "mass media"—has been to bring about during the present century, in large measure, the social equalization that Arnold so much desired.

Since the end of the last war one may say that there are in Britain practically speaking only two classes—a large and diversified middle class and a large and diversified working class—and the social and economic gap between the two is being steadily diminished.

In short, during the hundred years that have elapsed since Arnold published his essay on Equality, Great Britain, assisted by two World Wars, has carried out a bloodless political and social revolution, and is well on the way towards becoming an egalitarian society. If that is so, how—you may ask—can I say that the most significant tendencies of today, as compared with what I have called the old days, include pressures for increased liberty and equality? Hasn't the battle been won already? Where do we go from here?

My answer is that the tendencies I am talking about are concerned not with political but with personal relationships—not with relations between the individual and the State, or between groups, or between citizen and citizen, but with relations between human beings as human beings. Of course I am not denying that there are real political revolutionaries in Britain; we have over there, as I suppose you have over here, people who are so hostile to "bourgeois" society, and so impatient of "consensus" government and "repressive tolerance," that they would like to blow the whole Establishment sky-high. That is the professed aim of the Communist Party of Great Britain and of a miscellaneous crew of Marxists and Maoists, operating for the most part unorganized and underground. They are negligible in numbers and their influence doesn't amount, I should say, to a "significant tendency." But, apart from such dedicated extremists, there are very many, especially among the younger generation, who, without being politically minded or interested in revolutionary solutions, share the revolutionaries' hostility to the Establishment and their sense of alienation and personal frustration.

For the people I have in mind, equality, humanity, and liberty are not political or economic concepts. Equality is not an ideal to be realized by the overthrow of a governing class; it simply means that all hierarchies are unnatural, that no man is really good enough to claim superiority, as a human being, to any other man.

Their humanity is inspired not by any abstract

theory of the Brotherhood of Man, but by natural compassion, by an innate reluctance to inflict suffering on any fellow creature. As for liberty, they think of it simply as the individual's right to unrestrained self-expression, the right to "be yourself," to "do your own thing."

If one wants to see a realization of these ideals, one should look not to the Communist state, but to the hippy commune. Hippy communes are not a frequent feature of the English scene; it is not a national characteristic to carry things to extremes. But the ideals that inspire such a commune are shared and advocated—though not always consciously shared or explicitly advocated—by many of the younger generation in Britain today.

The younger generation! One of the things that differentiate the Britain of today from the Britain of yesterday is the prominence of the part now played on the national scene by the young, and the importance attached to what young people think, and what they say, and what they want.

What are the agencies that have brought about this increase in the prestige of the young? The process begins in the home and continues at school. First, the tendency towards increased humanity makes parents reluctant to impose their authority by force. In the old days disobedient children were punished by their parents, or by their nurses (today there are no longer nurses and nurseries: children live in close and continuous contact with their parents, and that itself is a social change of no small significance); today there is a revulsion against the very thought of punishment. Besides this, there are new theories, favored by educational psychologists, about the bringing up of children. Children, it is said, should be treated as reasonable beings; you must not give an order or state a fact without providing an explanation. "Because I say so"— words which in my youth seemed ample justification for a parental command—are never heard in England today, and the very word "obedience" has a sadly old-fashioned ring. Again, parents themselves, if their authority is challenged, are often at a loss to justify it. They no longer themselves believe in the foundations on which it is supposed to rest, and—partly out of natural honesty, and partly because educationists tell them that it is wrong to deceive a child—they won't put forward justifications that they don't themselves believe in. Things were very different in the old days. My father, I remember, taught me the Catechism and the Ten Commandments. I don't think he really believed in the authority of the Church, or of the Scriptures, but I never thought of challenging him on the matter, and anyhow the Commandments and all they stood for provided a sort of framework that helped to keep me in my place.

Schoolmasters and university authorities today

adopt the same humanitarian, egalitarian attitude as parents. Teaching and learning ought, we are told, to be looked on as a joint enterprise; the old-fashioned attitude of the university teacher, who not only instructed his pupils but cared for them and looked after them, is written off as "paternalism": "Don't speak of us as adolescents," said an indignant student in Oxford the other day, "we are *young adults.*" When they leave school or university, the young today are faced by no shortage of employment, and are no longer dependent economically upon their parents—"I shall cut you off with a shilling," "I shall turn you out of the house," are no longer threats with any force behind them.[2]

All this has given the young in Britain a collective self-consciousness, a sense of solidarity, and has promoted them to be, I won't say a power in the land, but a sort of Fourth Estate. And it is among the younger generation that you will see most clearly at work the tendencies that I suggest are among the most significant features of society in Britain today, the tendencies that you will see worked out to their extreme in a community of hippies.

The tendencies I am talking about are expressed

2. In England now, however, the "job market" is shrinking, and graduates are beginning to suffer from the general shortage of employment.

in the life-style nowadays adopted by the young in universities in Britain, and not only in universities. Let me give you the results of my own personal observation. I came back from London some twenty-five years ago, to live in Oxford. My windows look out on the High Street, the main thoroughfare of the city, thronged every day during term-time with students hurrying to and from lectures or strolling at ease with their friends during hours of leisure. The change that has come over the outward appearance of these young people during the last ten or fifteen years is phenomenal. When I say "phenomenal" I mean phenomenal in two senses: it is a remarkable, an almost incredible, transformation, and it is also an outward sign of an inner disposition. In the old days, the Oxford student presented the classic image of youth, clean-limbed and fresh-complexioned, decent in dress and graceful in bearing. Today, his place has been taken by a new breed of adolescent, shock-headed and disheveled, with hair that seems to have run to seed, hiding ears and neck in a whiskery overgrowth. Clad in patched jeans and dirty anoraks, they pad hand in hand, sometimes with bare feet, along the city pavements, horrible specimens of humanity. Of course, not all the young are like that; but that is, and has been for the last decade or so, the prevailing type.

What is it that impels so many decent, intelligent, and (no doubt) potentially attractive young people to cultivate the hirsute and the hispid, the scruffy and the unkempt, and to present such a loathsome exterior to each other and to the world at large?

Most of the young in Oxford, no doubt, if you asked them why they cultivated the uncouth, would be hard put to it to suggest a reason: they do it because the others do. But what was it that determined the trend, and what sustains it? Of course it is a challenge to bourgeois respectability, the "square," the conventional, the dark blue suit, the carefully rolled umbrella. But why does the challenge take this form? Why not extravagant eccentric elegance, like the aesthetes of the 1880s challenging Victorian conventionality? Plainly, the challenge of these young people goes deeper: they are protesting—whether they know it or not—not merely against middle-class respectability, against a particular sort of convention, but against all conventions alike; not against one class, but against the whole structure of society; they are not concerned with appearances, they are concerned, in a more serious sense, about the hypocrisy of a society that is itself so much concerned with appearances. "We attach," they are saying, "more importance to the purity of our motives and the nobility of our ideals than to the cleanliness of our bodies and the neatness of our clothes. We are giving the world a visual lesson in priorities." And it is significant that the types they personify, with their straggling locks, their bushy beards, their bare feet, are the primitive man and the early Christian —Robinson Crusoe and Jesus Christ—the noble savage, the wild man of the woods, and the prophet whose Kingdom is not of this world.

I shall explore later on the effect of their libertarian and humanitarian feelings: here what I am concerned with is their feeling for equality.

Equality! It is a topic appropriate, surely, to the year that marks the bicentenary of the signing of the Declaration of Independence: the first of the truths enunciated by the Founding Fathers was that all men are created equal.

Confronted with this sublimely confident assertion, I can only ask "What on earth does it mean? What did they think that it meant?" It is said to be self-evident. Well, it had better be—for surely there is no external evidence to support it. I cannot myself think of any sense of the word "equal" that will make the proposition true. Men—which I take it includes in this context all human beings—differ from each other almost infinitely in physical and intellectual attributes and potentialities: it would be more plausible to say that it is undeniable that no two men are created equal.

The phrase "created equal" seems to assume the

existence of a Divine Creator. Indeed, the Declaration goes on to say expressly that their Creator endowed men with certain inalienable rights, of which it offers examples. "Equal," then, may be intended to mean equal in the sight of God: they are equal in His eyes, and in judging them He will treat them on a basis of absolute equality, in accordance with His own standards, whatever those standards may be. This may be acceptable to people who believe in God, but it does not provide them with any guidance as to how they themselves are to regard, or to treat, their fellow men; and to people who don't believe in God, it is really no help at all.

What the authors of this famous sentence must surely have had in mind was not equality in the sight of God, but equality under the law of man— or, rather, equality by the law of man. I say "*by* the law" rather than "*under* the law," because to say that men should be equal under the law is almost a tautology: of course every law must be administered strictly in accordance with its provisions and without respect of persons; so much is implied in calling it a law. It goes without saying that those who administer a law must treat all who come before them as that law says they should be treated, without favor or discrimination. The assertion must mean more than that: it must mean that men should be equal *by law*, that the law itself, the substantive law, should disregard men's natural inequalities and treat them as though they were in fact equal; it must not discriminate between them. What sort of discrimination is it that is forbidden? Plainly the law can impose different taxes on people by reference to the size of their incomes; plainly it can impose different conditions for work in different kinds of industry; plainly it may enjoin, or forbid, men to do things over which they have control, and may punish (or reward) them for having done such things. What the law must not do (the Founding Fathers may have been saying) is to discriminate between persons by reference to attributes over which they have no control, such as their age, their sex, their race. Perhaps this was what the authors of the Declaration had in mind when they used the phrase "*created* equal"; they may have meant that the law should not discriminate between people by reference to attributes with which they were endowed by nature.

If that is what the proposition means, I can only ask, where are we to find the justification for it? Why, after all, should the laws of a country give equal rights to, and impose the same obligations on, lunatics and sane persons, children and adults, women and men, people of diverse races or nationalities? No religion, so far as I know, prescribes that the law shall treat these categories uniformly. To appeal to the rights of man is surely to beg the question: What are the rights of man? What are they based on? Natural law? What determines natural law? The general benefit of the community? But whether it benefits the community to give equal rights to these different categories is an empirical question.

Whatever they may have meant by their Declaration, it is instructive to observe how the Founding Fathers proceeded. Soon after drawing up the document, the men who signed it had to devise constitutions for the newly founded states. How far did they then put into practice the principle of equality so sublimely asserted in the Declaration? All men were created equal—yes! but slaves remained slaves, and slaves were excluded from the franchise, and along with slaves were excluded women, minors, servants, non-whites, Roman Catholics, and Jews.

In a recent lecture in Oxford, Professor J. P. Greene, of Johns Hopkins University, put forward an interesting explanation of this apparent contradiction of principle by practice. He suggested that the Founding Fathers, when they proclaimed the equality of man, were more concerned with the definition of man than with the definition of equality. "Equality" meant simply an equal share in electing the government: every qualified citizen must have a vote. The question was, who was to qualify as a citizen? Professor Greene argues most persuasively, and with an impressive array of supporting evidence from speeches and pamphlets by politicans and controversialists belonging to the period of the Revolution—that the signatories of the Declaration of Independence were perpetuating the laws concerning the franchise that their colonial forebears derived from the mother country: to qualify as a voter under English law as it then stood, a man must have a stake in the country—he must have a property qualification—and he must be in a position to cast his vote without dependence upon others. Hence the exclusion of married women, of slaves, of servants, of infants (it probably was the practical truth in those days, that if you gave a vote to a woman or to a slave, you were simply giving an extra vote to the husband of the woman, or the owner of the slave) and also of Roman Catholics, who were thought to be subject to their spiritual directors. Besides this, the English law said, a man must be, in a special, civic sense, "virtuous": he must enjoy not merely independence of others—owners, masters, husbands, parents— but mastery of self, freedom from internal subjection to his own passions. This criterion obviously excluded the insane and criminals; it was held also to exclude others who had such natural or cultural disabilities that they were incapable of self-control, and therefore lacked the capacity to attain the virtue and the competence that would qualify them for full civic status in society. Hence, I am sorry to say, it was felt necessary to exclude from the franchise not only slaves and married women, on the ground of their dependent status, but also, as lacking in the requisite civic competence, all women, even if unmarried, non-whites, even if free, and Jews.

So much for the political theories, or some of the political theories, that have actuated egalitarians in the past. My excursion into that field has been rapid and superficial; I embarked upon it only in order to point a contrast, a contrast between the political egalitarianism of yesterday and the very different and quite unpolitical egalitarianism that, if I am right, inspires many of the younger generation, and not only the younger generation, today. What they are concerned about is not political equality—"One man, one vote"—nor equality in the eye of the law—equal rights for unequal people. Such equalities do no more than organize and regulate the existing social and economic hierarchies, with the strong, the astute, and the ambitious climbing to the top by the ladder of social mobility. They are not champions of the oppressed; they are simply reluctant to assert or to recognize the existence of superiority, they hate hierarchies, they abominate the conception of an élite. "Meritocracy" is for them a dirty word—not because it is a horrible etymological hybrid, but because, like the word "aristocracy," it suggests a set of superior people. And the fact that "meritocrats" achieve their superior position because they are lucky enough to have been endowed by nature with particular abilities or advantages makes matters no better—even if it doesn't make them worse.

Few of those who are moved by this anti-hierarchical impulse have analyzed it or thought out its implications. But it has a practical effect: one can see it at work in several fields.

First, in education: in schools and universities. There is, in England, an increasing body of opinion that is against publishing the results of examinations. If you publish examination results, it is said, you clearly advertise the superiority of the successful candidates and the inferiority of those who fail, and that humiliates the unsuccessful and is apt to give the successful swollen heads—and that must be bad for both alike. Even if the results are not published, the fact that candidates are graded is enough to register the painful contrast between success and failure, between superiority and inferiority; so it is proposed that examinations themselves should be abolished. Their abolition would not only make it more difficult to differentiate unkindly between one student and another, it would at the same time be a step towards abolishing the invidious distinction between the teacher and the taught. Invidious —for the process of learning is felt to be a co-operative endeavor, in which all should participate on an equal footing.

The huge and rapid extension of university education that has taken place in England since the War has led to applications from large numbers of less well qualified students for admission to the universities, and this in turn has led to pressure for lowering the standards for admission, and lowering the standards demanded for a degree. The standards must be shaped to the people, said a progressive don in Oxford the other day, rather than the people to the standards. The appeal was based on egalitarian and humanitarian grounds: it isn't the fault of the student if he is slower witted than his rivals—moreover, he may not have enjoyed so good an education at school. Perhaps his parents couldn't afford to send him to a better school: should he be made to suffer for deficiencies that are no fault of his? Should a university cater for, and strive to produce, an academic élite? Should it not shape its standards so as to cater for the less fortunate of its students? My own answer to these questions would be unambiguous: I would say that being an élitist establishment is nothing to be ashamed of; excellence may not be a matter for pride, but it is never a matter for regret. Universities and schools that cast away their inheritance, not because they cease to believe in its value but out of deference to egalitarian pressure, are betraying an intellectual trust and becoming parties to the most recent manifestation of *la trahison des clercs.*

Besides education, there is another field in which one can see at work the desire to suppress distinctions, and so to eliminate superiorities and inferiorities: that is, the field of Art. The very concept of Fine Art is as repugnant to the egalitarian as it is to the revolutionary: he abhors, and would repudiate, the sort of "Civilisation" that was the subject of a famous series of lectures by Lord Clark. The notorious pronouncement of John Lennon, the Beatle —"The Mona Lisa is a load of crap"—is relevant here: it should be interpreted, I think, as expressing not a specific aesthetic judgment, but a desire to repudiate the traditional culture of the West and to reject in its totality the conception of Fine Art.

"Down with the past!" cries John Cage, the man who makes his music out of silence, "Down with the masterpiece!" "Down"—it surely follows— "with the Great Artist!" And from there it is a short step to "Down with the artist!" The artist is a man with special gifts that can be fully appreciated only by the limited number of people who are born with, and have been able to cultivate, aesthetic sensibility and a special power of discrimination.

There was a significant dialogue between the poet Stephen Spender and a student rebel, when Spender was in Paris at the time of the rebellion in the Cité Universitaire of Nanterre. Spender asked the young rebel, meaning to be friendly, whether he was an artist. "Am I an artist?" was the indignant reply, "What do you mean? Everyone is an artist." Yes, we are all artists now: hence "audience participation" and Pop Art, the "happening," the *objet trouvé*, and the impersonal works of art produced by aleatory machines.

A similar tendency shows itself in the field of sex. Many of the young in Britain want, it seems, to mask the difference between male and female by putting into circulation as human currency a unisexual (but not hermaphroditic) type. A generation ago, it used to be said jokingly in Oxford that, what with men letting their hair grow long and women wearing trousers, soon you wouldn't be able to tell one sex from another. What was then said in jest has now become the sober truth. Every day one sees in the streets more and more young people with their hair about their shoulders, epicene in dress, and physically distinguishable as to sex only by profusion of beard on the one hand or, on the other, by protuberance of breast.

Why do they do it? Not just out of a desire for novelty, not simply in order to provoke their elders —that would be altogether too facile an explanation. Nor is it intended as a demonstration of their belief in equal rights for the two sexes. Whether they know it or not, the style has for them a purpose both more serious and more significant: by camouflaging the secondary differences between the sexes, it emphasizes their common humanity.[3]

Sex equality is taken for granted: what they are insisting upon is sexual indifference. It is a natural consequence of this depreciation of sexual difference that sexual activity itself should be for the young today a less serious and specialized affair than it was for their elders—less personal, less "genital" (in current jargon) and more "polymorphic," an everyday incident, a recreation, like mixed hockey in the past, an activity that satisfies at the same time the desire for comradeship and the desire for play. Love, for them, means a diffused benevolence, which finds expression in altruistic concern for the "alienated" and the oppressed, and also in the impersonal, half-mystical, love of the "love-in," a gathering where, as at the *agapai* of the early Christians, everybody enjoys a loving association, of one sort or another, with everybody else. The one thing that love does not mean to them, it seems, is the mysterious, possessive, devastating personal passion, known to the Greeks as *eros*, the intense preoccupation—a favorite theme of so many novelists and poets—of one individual person with another.

Too much of a good thing! It is surely a good thing that a new generation should grow up sin-

3. This is the feeling that inspires the chorus of the Unisex Anthem:
Raise the clarion call again;
Beards for women, breasts for men!

cere, honest, humble, high-minded, compassion-
ate, humane; opposed to the oppression of one
class, or one race, by another, to hostility between
nations, to the use of force, to war. Honesty,
humility, compassion—are these really things that
you can have too much of?

Well, yes: I think that you can have too much of
them, in the sense that you can pay too dearly for
their indulgence: you may find that by indulging in
them without restraint you have sacrificed civilization itself. Civilization depends for its existence
upon maintaining the authority of the law; the
authority of the law cannot be maintained without
the application of force—and force means suffering. Compassion is not enough.

Civilized society depends, likewise, upon the
maintenance of a highly artificial system of conventions:"Civilization," said J. M. Keynes, "is a thin
and precarious crust erected by the personality and
the will of a very few and only maintained by rules
and conventions skilfully put across and guilefully
preserved." Not long ago I read a *graffito* inscribed
upon an Oxford wall: "Smash hypocrisy now!"
was the message that it carried. But hypocrisy, in
the sense intended by the author of that message, is
the cement that holds society together: "smash"
hypocrisy and you destroy civilization. Honesty
is not enough.

Finally, civilization depends upon the recognition and the cultivation of excellence, and excellence implies superiority. Equality means the denial of superiority, and ultimately the denial of diversity, for every difference between one human being and another may be made the ground for asserting a superiority or an inferiority on one side or the other. Absolute equality between human beings, if it were attainable, would mean, as it does in the world of mathematics, absolute identity. Against such a conclusion, even that egalitarian nation, the French, have lodged their protest: *Vive la différence!* And Matthew Arnold, if he saw the lengths to which his doctrine is being pressed today, would surely change his message and bid us "Choose inequality!"

# Humanity

There are, as it seems to me, several tendencies that make themselves felt in society today, in Great Britain and, I suspect, elsewhere in the West, that are undeniably good, but can be overvalued; if we pay too highly for them, I suggest, and if we let them carry us too far, the world will be a worse place. One of these tendencies is a tendency towards increased humanity.

When I use the word humanity, of course I don't mean the condition of being human; I mean the attribute of being humane—humaneness of disposition. Of course I think that it is a good thing that human beings should be humane, that they should be disposed to be kind and gentle to each other and to all living creatures, that they should shrink from imposing their wills by force upon their fellow men and from inflicting pain or injury upon them, and that they should seek to promote this disposition among human beings generally. Humanity in this sense is a good thing; it distinguishes us from brutes and barbarians, and the more successfully we cultivate our humane disposition, the less like brutes and barbarians we shall be.

Can we have too much of it? That is the question. When we are judging individuals, can we safely say that the kinder, the gentler, the more humane a person is, the better he is as a member of society? And when we compare one society with another, can we say that the more humane it is in its customs and its laws, the better a society it is? I think that that would be to go too far. I think it would be to over-value one good thing at the expense of others. And I think that today, at least in Great Britain, we are in danger of doing just that—indeed, that in certain areas we are doing it already.

It is a bad thing to be hard: but it does not follow that it is a good thing to be soft—and there are situations in which it is a good thing, a necessary thing, to be tough. A hard man is a man deficient in human sympathy; a tough man is a man who has his sympathy under control. It is toughness, not hardness, that I am contending for.

There are two reasons why our tender-heartedness needs to be supplemented by toughness. First, because someone who can't face the fact of suffering cannot adequately meet the responsibilities that fall to his lot as a member of society. Second, because—if it is judged by strictly practical and utilitarian tests, by its consequences, its effects upon society—the refusal to countenance the deliberate imposition of force and the deliberate infliction of pain may prove to be self-defeating: it may well produce a greater volume of suffering in the long run than it saves in the short run; in order to spare our mind's eye the image of immediate suffering, we may so act that others, and ourselves also, will suffer more in the end.

I said that a man who can't face the fact of suffering cannot meet his responsibilities as a member of society. Let me explain what I mean, and let me begin my explanation by offering you a very homely illustration.

I remember my mother telling me, after I was grown up, about a small boy who couldn't bear, in the nursery, to see or to think of his brother or his sisters being punished. He hated it so much that sometimes, when a misdemeanor of theirs was discovered, he would pretend that it was he that was the culprit: it really hurt him less if he himself was punished. Now these childish misdemeanors must have been very trivial, and the punishments far from severe, so the self-sacrifice of that small boy— if indeed it was self-sacrifice—wasn't very much to be proud of. But was it anything to be proud of at all? I ask the question with some concern, because I have to confess that I was that small boy myself; and I must say that I still shrink from the contemplation, even with the mind's eye, of somebody being hurt or humiliated. But wasn't my apparent altruism in my nursery days really a kind of selfishness or self-indulgence? The thing that worried me, was it really the suffering of my brother or my sisters? Was it not rather my own suffering at the thought of theirs? However that may have been, I was certainly giving more weight to my own feelings than to considerations of truth or—and here is the real point—of social justice and social good, of what was right and fair all round in the small world of the nursery.

That may give you a clue to what I mean when I say that a man who refuses to contemplate the infliction of pain, or the imposition of force, cannot meet his responsibilities as a member of society.

The man who allows himself to be guided entirely by the tenderness of his heart will not only decline to be himself a party to the imposition of force or the infliction of pain, he will oppose such imposition or infliction by others; and, if he is consistent, he will use his vote and his influence against laws and practices that involve the imposition of discipline by force. Such a man would find it impossible—surely—to run a prison, or a hospital, or a business, or a school, or indeed a family; and it is difficult to see how any of those institutions—or indeed any civilized society—could survive if the doctrines of pure humanitarianism were consistently applied. That is why I say that humanity, though a good thing, is a good thing of which you can have too much, and that a man who cannot face the fact of suffering cannot meet his responsibilities as a member of society.

And that leads me to my second reason for saying that tenderness must be supplemented by toughness: unalloyed, unrestrained humanity may well produce in the long run more suffering than it saves.

Let us look at some of the areas in which humanitarianism is put to the test. Take the issue of war and peace—or, rather, of war and pacifism. We prefer, surely, peace-loving nations to warlike, militaristic, nations; we abhor force as the arbiter of international disputes. We abhor it, but should we abjure it? Suppose two countries are threatened by a third, a totalitarian, militaristic power. One of the two, passively resisting, allows itself to be over-run; the other goes to war in its own defense. Do we applaud the first and deplore the second? In the country that goes to war, the individual citizen will, of course, be faced with a personal problem: is he, or is he not, to fight? Do we prefer the pacifist, the man who declines military service on conscientious grounds, or the man who joins the armed forces and takes his part in the bombing and destroying of the enemy? We may respect the pacifist, but should we conclude that the more pacifists there are in a nation, the more civilized that nation will be? By refusing to go to war, it may simply be signing its own death-warrant as a civilized society.

I suggested that there was in Britain today a pronounced, perhaps even an excessive, tendency towards increased humanity; I don't think that this applies, however, to the general attitude concerning war: I doubt whether the doctrine of pure pacifism has many adherents in the country. The British have never been a militaristic nation, and people today are of course very conscious of the unspeakable horrors of modern warfare. They abolished peace-time National Military Service about twenty years ago, and I don't believe that any Government now would think of re-introducing it. Still, one may ask: "If the country were faced with a clear threat of military aggression, could the Government depend on the response it would get if it declared war, mobilized the Army, and drafted civilians into it? Would there be, on any appreciable scale, a refusal to fight, a refusal to be drafted?" I don't think so. Memories of 1939, and the threat of Nazi invasion, and the Battle of Britain, are still potent, at least among older people —though when I talk to students who were born, as all today's students were, after the War was over, I sometimes wonder what would be their response to a call-up. "Wouldn't you have joined up against Hitler?" I ask—and Hitler seems to be to them about as real a figure, about as much of a bogey-man, as Napoleon Bonaparte.

I have given you my opinion, for what it is worth, about the state of feeling in Great Britain. How it is with you over here, I do not know. I am not so rash as to invite discussion of the issues raised by the war from which this country has recently—shall I say?—rescued itself. Still less will I presume to pass judgment, one way or the other, upon any of those issues. But I can't help indulging in one speculation that arises from that war and that seems to me germane to the point that I am now trying to make. It is this. A vast majority of those who opposed the war, and a vast majority of those who declined to be drafted into the armed forces, must surely have been actuated by two convictions, right or wrong: first, that it was not a just war; and, second, that the country had never really been consulted on the question whether the war should be waged or not. So strongly, I imagine, were these convictions held by most of those concerned, that very few of them can have stayed to ask themselves the question "Would I have taken up arms and fought if I had thought the war to be a just one?", or the question "Would I have been prepared to fight if I had thought it an unjust war, but it was the clear and declared opinion of the majority of the nation that it was a just war?" In short, the questions "Is there such a thing as a just war?" and "What makes a war a just war?" were questions that, in their view of the actual situation, simply did not arise.

And I would add this reflection: it may well be that the recent experience of this country has made it more likely that, if the question of going to war should again present itself in practice, the rising generation would answer: "There is no such thing as a just war." The experience that this country has been through has given war—so to speak—a bad name, and has strengthened the tendency to pure unadulterated pacifism. The humanitarian may say that this much good, at least, has come of evil: the rationalist, the tough-minded man, may not be so sure.

The problem I have so far put before you with regard to war is a straightforward one—in effect: "Would you be a pacifist, or would you fight?" Let me add two special problems, where the issues are not so simple.

Suppose that you had been serving in the war against Hitler and that you held a prisoner who, to your knowledge, possessed information that would ensure and accelerate an Allied victory: to what lengths would you think it permissible to go in order to extract that information from him? Is there any form of torture, mental or physical, at which you would draw the line? Or suppose that just a touch of torture, a mild beating-up, would suffice; would you hold that even the slightest pressure was impermissible? Remember that if you don't extract the information, the war may continue for months or years, with hundreds of thousands of lives lost on both sides, and that it may end in victory for the Nazis. Assume also that all you did would be done in secret: no-one, or virtually no-one, need ever know about it. Faced by that problem, how should the true humanitarian act?

My other problem is a more topical one. It arises

out of the activities of hijackers, who declare that, unless their demands are satisfied, they will kill the hostages that they have taken. Suppose that a hundred innocent persons are held captive, and threatened with death, unless half-a-dozen political prisoners are released. What attitude should be adopted by the Governments concerned? Are they to allow the innocent victims to be killed, perhaps one by one over a long and agonizing period, or are they to save their lives by fulfilling the hijackers' demands, however far-reaching and however outrageous? I do not suggest what the answer should be; but I cannot help pointing out that the extreme humanitarian in such a case would be in favor of saving the lives of the hostages, at whatever cost to the countries concerned, and to civilization generally.

Let me turn now to another field. The humanitarian tendency I have been speaking of reveals itself in the sphere of law-enforcement, and enforcement of discipline generally, especially in people's feelings about capital punishment and corporal punishment as sanctions under the criminal law, and about corporal punishment as a means of enforcing discipline in schools.

It is ten years since the death penalty was abolished in Great Britain. I have taken part, during those years, in quite a number of debates, formal and informal, on the issue "Should capital punishment be re-introduced?" and my experience is that it is difficult to find people, at any rate among academics and intellectuals, and especially among the younger generation, who will defend the death penalty. During that period, crimes of violence, including murder, have dramatically increased, and I have no doubt that if a referendum of the whole population were taken, there would be a decisive majority in favor of restoring the death penalty for murder and probably (but I am not so sure about this) a majority in favor of bringing back corporal punishment for particularly monstrous crimes of violence. But I am equally sure that no Government, whether Socialist or Conservative, will re-introduce either capital or corporal punishment in Great Britain.

You may ask why there is (if I am right) this divergence between the electorate as a whole and its representatives in Parliament. The answer, I think, is that on questions of social policy, where popular opinion is apt to change slowly, Parliament is always, or almost always, in advance of the country at large; indeed it is a claim regularly made on behalf of the House of Commons that on such questions, it should, and does, give a lead to the nation; so it is not surprising that the humanitarian tendency that I detect among academics and intellectuals and the Left generally in England on the question of capital punishment should be reflected in the House of Commons, even though (if I am right) the mass of the people is not in agreement with them. The question, I suggest, is whether this is not an issue on which Parliament, pushed too far by a humanitarian tendency, is leading the country in the wrong direction.

I don't want to argue the case for or against capital punishment under English law, still less under American law, about which I know nothing, or next to nothing: Is it a cruel and unusual punishment? If it is recognized by the law, should it be mandatory? What are the requirements of due process?—on all such questions I am entirely ignorant. But capital punishment is a very topical issue, I gather, in the United States; it provides a test case, so to speak, for the humanitarian; and I should like to look at it, for a moment, not from the point of view of the lawyer, but from the point of view of the ordinary man.

The plea that is usually the first to be put forward by the opponents of capital punishment is an appeal to the sanctity of human life. "Sanctity"— what does that mean? It has a religious ring. But what religion is being appealed to? Buddhism, I believe, regards *all* life, not merely human life, as sacred. But to those who are not Buddhists the religious appeal will surely ring hollow. Christianity, certainly, does not forbid the taking of human life—indeed, it teaches us that our earthly life is something on which we should not put too high a value. I suspect that when people appeal to the sanctity of human life in this context, all they really mean is that human life is a very valuable, a uniquely valuable, thing. No doubt it is. But whatever the value of a human life, two human lives must—other things being equal—be more valuable than one. Therefore, it must be right—other things, I repeat, being equal—to sacrifice one life to save two or more. And to save the lives of potential victims is one of the purposes of capital punishment. That leads to the question of deterrence.

Of course, one of the purposes of all criminal sanctions, one of the reasons for inflicting severe punishments upon delinquents, is that the punishment should deter other potential criminals from committing similar offenses. And here I think that the horror and revulsion that makes sensitive, humane people want to abolish the death penalty affords one of the strongest arguments for retaining it. For it *is* very horrible, dramatically horrible; and it is through this horror that it may act upon potential murderers. It operates at—so to speak—two levels.

Take the poisoner, or the bank robber. Both plan their crimes. Both make calculations. And two principal factors in their calculations are: first, how likely it is that they will be caught; and, second, what will happen to them if they are. The thought that the punishment for murder is death may well be decisive in persuading the intending poisoner not to administer the arsenic, and the intending bank robber not to carry a gun.

That is first-degree deterrence. By second-degree deterrence I mean the deterrent force of capital punishment operating, not by affecting the conscious thoughts of individuals tempted to kill, but by building up in the community, over a long period of time, a deep feeling of peculiar abhorrence for the crime of murder. I quote from the report of a Royal commission on Capital Punishment set up in England some years ago: "This widely diffused effect on the moral consciousness of society is impossible to assess, but it must be at least as important as any direct part which the death penalty may play as a deterrent in the calculations of potential murderers."

So much for first-degree and second-degree deterrence. Of course there are *crimes passionels*— murders that are committed in hot blood, under the influence of sudden overwhelming passion or of intoxication. In such cases, the murderer will not be affected, let alone deterred, by the thought of the punishment to which his act renders him liable: he simply will not think about it. But that is only one category of murder; the cold-blooded murderer, on the other hand, will surely take into account the penalty he is liable to suffer if he is caught.

It isn't easy to say how far the death penalty actually operates as a deterrent, either in the first or in the second degree, or to estimate how much difference, if it does deter, its abolition would make in the murder rate. Some European countries abolished it many years ago, and some of them have reintroduced it. There are voluminous statistics recording the murder rate in all, or almost all, those countries before and after abolition, and these statistics are appealed to in support of their case both by those who oppose the death penalty and by those who defend it. A confusing factor is that many countries abandoned the death penalty in practice, and began automatically to reprieve all, or almost all, convicted murderers, many years before they abolished it formally: this casts doubt on the significance of the statistics, and of the graphs extrapolated from the statistics, which seem to indicate that abolition made no difference to the rate: in those countries the actual abolition was a "non-event."

The opponents of the death penalty make the main plank in their case the contention that it is not a uniquely efficient deterrent—if, indeed, it deters at all—and that prolonged imprisonment would be just as efficacious. They have other practical arguments besides: it is irrevocable, and you may have made a mistake; and if you execute an innocent man, you can't bring him back to life—to which supporters of capital punishment reply that the law is hedged about with such safeguards, at any rate in England, that the execution of an innocent man is not a practical possibility.

Other arguments—still less cogent, in my opinion—are put forward: the process of carrying out an execution, it is said, brutalizes the members of the prison staff who have to take part in it, and has a deplorable psychological effect on the other inmates of the prison where it takes place.

As I have said, I don't want to evaluate the arguments on one side and the other, or to attempt to decide between them, because I think that all this arguing, as far as the opponents of capital punishment are concerned, is simply shadow-boxing. What really counts with them, or most of them, is not reason or argument, but a deep feeling of revulsion from the whole thing—a humanitarian feeling, the feeling that, in a civilized country in the twentieth century, the State can't kill a man in cold blood. Forget all the arguments based on the brutalization of the prison staff or the possibility that an innocent man may be executed; forget deterrence; assume, if you like, that you will deter twenty murderers by electrocuting or guillotining or hanging one guilty murderer—you just can't do it; it is simply barbaric, and there's an end to it.

Ah, but—the defenders of capital punishment

will reply—an execution today isn't the barbarous affair that it was in the bad old days, not much more than a hundred years ago, when men were hanged in public, and crowds gathered outside the prison to enjoy the spectacle, and drink flowed freely, and a cheer was raised when the executioner pulled the bolt that launched the prisoner into eternity. It is all very different now: it all takes place in privacy, and the whole thing is conducted with decorum and dispatch.

That is quite true. Today an execution is a very scientific, very clinical affair. Let me read you a description from a little book, *A Life for a Life*, written by Sir Ernest Gowers, a civil servant who was Chairman of the Royal Commission from whose report I have quoted. Here is Sir Ernest Gowers' account of what happens (or what used to happen) at an execution in Britain in modern, up-to-date, conditions: "The Under-Sheriff, to whom the High Sheriff usually assigns this part of his duties, arrives at the prison about twenty minutes before the time of the execution—it is always 8 o'clock in the morning. A few minutes before it he goes with the Governor and the Medical Officer to the execution chamber. The executioner and his assistant will by then be waiting outside the door of the condemned cell, together with the Chief Officer and the officer detailed to conduct the prisoner to the gallows. The Under-Sheriff gives a signal, and the executioner and the officers enter the cell. The executioner pinions the prisoner's arms behind his back. He is then escorted to the execution chamber, with one officer on each side and the Chaplain preceding. The Under-Sheriff, Governor and Medical Officer enter the chamber by another door.

"The prisoner is placed on the trap on a spot marked in white chalk, in such a position that his feet are directly across the division of the doors. The executioner draws a white cap over his head and places the noose round his neck; the assistant executioner pinions his legs. As soon as the executioner sees that all is ready, he goes to the lever and pulls it. It is all done very quickly. The time between the entry of the executioner into the condemned cell and the pulling of the lever is normally about ten seconds; in a few prisons, where the execution chamber does not adjoin the condemned cell, it may be longer, but seldom more than twenty-five seconds." What, you may ask, could be more civilized or more expeditious than that?

Yes: I know it is all conducted in the most civilized fashion, but does that make it any the more acceptable to the humanitarian? In a way it makes it more ghastly.

Perhaps I might here tell a story of a personal

experience, the nearest I ever got to attending an execution myself. It was more than twenty years ago; I was visiting an old college friend of mine who lived in the County of Norfolk. He lived alone with his mother, in a beautiful old house, the ancestral home of his family, not luxuriously but in great comfort. He was a scholarly person, who edited eighteenth-century authors and wrote articles on local history in archaeological magazines; gentle, kind, considerate; the sort of man who wouldn't hurt a fly. He met me at the railway station at Norwich in his very comfortable car. I hadn't seen him for some time, and as we drove through the quiet Norfolk countryside I asked him what news he had of himself. He said he had recently been appointed Under-Sheriff of the County of Norfolk, a post which involved him from time to time in formal ceremonial duties. The Queen had visited Norwich not long before, and he had had to be in attendance. "It all went off very well," said my friend. It occurred to me to ask whether it wouldn't fall to him as Under-Sheriff to be in attendance at executions, if any prisoners were condemned to death at the Norwich Assizes; I said that I hoped he hadn't had to undergo that experience—I thought (though I didn't say so) that he simply wouldn't have been able to face it. My friend said that when he accepted the post of Under-Sheriff, the Sheriff had offered to appoint a deputy to attend at the prison if by any chance an execution should take place during his term of office. "But," said my friend, "I declined the appointment of a deputy. I felt that, if the occasion arose, it was my duty to go through with it. It would be a valuable experience." "Well," I said, "I hope it won't fall to your lot." "As a matter of fact," he replied, "there was an execution in Norwich last week," and he explained that it had been a double execution: two young men had been condemned to death at the Assizes; each, in a fit of passion, had murdered his girl; and it was thought fitting that they should be hanged together. They consented, and so it took place; "I think they really preferred it that way," said my friend. "But were you actually in the execution chamber?" I asked. "Of course," he answered. "I suppose it's a big room," I said, hopefully, "and you were at the far end of it?" "Oh, no," he replied, "it's a very small room; I wasn't more than a few feet away." I didn't know what to say; there was a pause. "It all went off very well," said my friend, "I was home in time for breakfast.... Ah, here we are"—and he brought the car to a halt in front of his ancestral mansion, where his old mother was waiting for him on the steps. My friend, I repeat, was a very humane man. But it occurred to me that he was also a very tough man, tougher than I had supposed. I looked at him with admiration, an admiration not unmixed with horror. Horror—why?

Well, let me quote some verses by Ralph Hodgson, an English poet who migrated to the United States towards the end of his life, and died in Ohio ten years or so ago:

> To hang a man:
> To fit the cap,
> And fix the rope,
> And slide the bar,
> And let him drop.
> I know, I know:
> What can you do!
> You have no choice,
> You're driven to;
> You can't be soft—
> A man like that;
> But Oh it seems—
> I don't know what—
> To hang a man!

Well, you can't argue against that: it is a matter of feeling. Statistics about the deterrent effect of the death penalty, even if conclusive in its favor, are irrelevant—you just can't hang a man in England today: that is what the opponents of capital punishment, I believe—or nine out of ten of them—are saying. Suppose you could prove that by executing, and only by executing, half-a-dozen murderers a year you would save the lives of half-a-dozen, or a dozen, or a score, or even a hundred innocent victims—night watchmen, bank guards, policemen, prison warders, or old ladies murdered so that the murderer could steal their savings—you still shouldn't do it. Better that a hundred innocent human beings should be murdered than that half-a-dozen guilty murderers should be executed. That is the attitude of the humanitarians.

Do you agree with them? I do not. But I have to confess that if it could be proved that torture—the thumbscrew, the rack, boiling oil, or a more painful method of putting people to death, say, burning them alive—would increase the deterrent effect of the death penalty, and save a few more innocent lives every year, I don't think I could bring myself to support a law introducing such punishments. And my reason, if it is a reason, for taking up that position is just the same as the humanitarian's reason, if it is a reason, for opposing capital punishment: torturing people in cold blood is something you can't do in a civilized country today.

Let me now turn from the criminal law to the field of education. I don't mean university education: in a university the problem of discipline—what you do to people if they break the rules—only arises in exceptional circumstances: there are so few rules to break. I mean education in schools; and the schools I want to draw your special attention to, because they provide the most striking illustration of the point I want to make, are those private schools in Great Britain—misleadingly called "Public Schools"—where the sons of what used to be called the upper classes, and of the middle classes, are educated between the ages of twelve and eighteen. They are most of them ancient foundations; some of them date back to the days before the Reformation; some of them were founded during the succeeding centuries; all of them are independent of control by the State.

Side by side with the Public Schools there are the State Schools, set up during the last hundred years under a series of Education Acts, which are financed and controlled by the State and provide a compulsory education for children whose parents can't afford, or don't wish, to send them to private schools. (The Socialist Government now in power is trying, in the interests of "equality," to eliminate private, independent schools by penal taxation, so that everyone will have the same education provided by the State. But that is another story).

How do State Schools and Public Schools in Britain deal with the problem of enforcing discipline? To appreciate the answer to this question, one must look at the different conditions under which the two kinds of school carry out their task.

The State School is a building comprising classrooms with an adjoining playground, where children go every morning to be taught, returning to their families when afternoon school is over. Enforcing discipline in such a school means little more than keeping order in class; it is effected by a teacher, by means of personality, reinforced on occasions, not very menacingly, and not very frequently, I suspect, by a cane: "Hold out your hand!" in the presence of the class—that sort of thing.

For the Public School, discipline presents a very different problem, at once more complex and more difficult. To understand the difference, you must bear in mind that the Public Schools are boarding schools, in which boys and masters—I say "boys and masters" because the Public Schools are, by and large, all-male establishments—live together, day in, day out, in a little self-contained world, governed by customs and traditions which vary from one school to another, but have a common stamp—"the Public School stamp"—which they imprint on the pupils who pass through them. The phrase "a Public School man" has, or used to have, a definite social, not to say snobbish, implication. The Public Schools, until Victorian days, were a sort of playground for the children of the gentry and the aristocracy. Then came Dr. Arnold, the father of Matthew Arnold, who was Headmaster of Rugby School in the 1830s, and who will be familiar to any one who has read *Tom Brown's School Days* or Lytton Strachey's *Eminent Victorians*.

Largely as a result of the influence of Dr. Arnold and the model that he created at Rugby, the Public Schools became the training ground of the British governing class, so long as we had a governing class, and educated the civil servants who ran the British Empire, so long as there was a British Empire.

The backbone of the Public School system was—and still is—the prefectorial system. The masters, of course, do the teaching and make the rules, and ultimate power resides with them; the prefects are senior boys to whom the master delegates a measure of his authority. This teaches them how to wield power responsibly, and is (or is supposed to be) an important part of their education.

Together with the prefectorial system goes the system of "fagging." The prefects are served and waited upon by "fags," junior boys, usually in their first year, who have to perform menial tasks for their seniors, the prefects—running errands for them, cleaning their shoes, dusting their books, making tea and washing up, fetching and carrying, calling them in the morning, and so on. To keep the fags in order, and to ensure that they carry out their duties efficiently, the prefects can inflict punishments, and the commonest and most effective form of punishment—anyhow until recently—was beating. The instrument employed was regularly a cane; in my old school it was an ashplant, called a ground ash. Really serious offenses would be dealt with by the housemaster, and a housemaster's beating was a solemn affair—less painful, perhaps, than a prefect's beating (the prefects were often chosen for strength and athletic ability) but a more impressive occasion; a prefect's beating was an everyday occurrence. (I don't mean that someone was beaten every day, but simply that it was by no means a rare event). It was a convenient and acceptable form of punishment, expeditious, humiliating, exemplary—and often preferred by the victim to such alternatives as tedious periods of detention, a troublesome imposition, or a suspension of privileges.

Of course this system depended, if it was to work fairly and well, upon the character and morale of the prefects, and upon adequate supervision by the housemaster. In a good house, all went well. But the system gave plenty of scope, in a bad house, to a prefect who was a bully or a sadist. From time to time there were exposures of abuses of their power on the part of the prefects: you can read about the kind of thing that happened in novels of school life and autobiographies of sensitive men whose personalities were scarred and marred—or who believe that their personalities were scarred and marred—by the brutalities and the injustices—or what seemed to them the brutalities and the injustices—that they had undergone at the hands of their seniors in their schooldays. But, on the whole, the system worked well. Most old Public School men, or at least most Public School men of the older generations, will tell you "I was beaten pretty often when I was at Rugby (or Charterhouse, or Harrow, or wherever it was they went to), and it never did me any harm." "In fact" they will often go on to say, "it did me all the good in the world." Personally, if I were cross-examined about my own school experience, I should have to admit that I belong to this latter class: I was beaten pretty often, and I don't believe a beating ever did me any harm.

Having said so much, perhaps I owe it to myself to add that, when I became a prefect, I never beat anyone at all. This was not due to conscientious scruples on my part. I shouldn't have enjoyed beating anyone, and I managed to get on without doing it.

What is the attitude towards corporal punishment adopted today in the Public Schools? To judge from what is happening in my own old school—and from what I hear about other Public Schools—the prefectorial system, the exercise of authority by big boys over smaller boys, is being eroded, and in particular—and this is the point I want to bring home—the "prefect's beating" is practically a thing of the past. It is on its way out, if it isn't actually extinct. And why? Not because the victims have risen in rebellion on the grounds of justice or egalitarian feeling, not because the small boys refuse to allow themselves to be beaten, but because the big boys, the prefects, decline to beat them: the practice has gone out, it is out of fashion, it is contrary to the humanitarian tendency of the day.

It is out of fashion, not only with the prefects, but with the masters also. "It hurts me more than it hurts you," old-fashioned parents or schoolmasters used to say, as they applied the birch-rod to the tender bodies of their unfortunate offspring or pupils. If the remark was quoted against them, as it often was, that was because it was thought to be insincere: if they didn't actually enjoy beating their children, at least—or so it was thought—it gave them satisfaction to administer what they believed to be a healthy discipline.

So it was in the old days. Today, "enlightened" parents and schoolmasters, at least in Britain, rarely chastise children: to do so really would hurt them more than it would hurt the victims. But—I can't help asking—if that is their reason for refraining from enforcing discipline, are they not really being self-indulgent at the expense of those committed to their charge? "Spare the rod, and spoil the child," said the old adage. I don't know whether it contains a truth; I wouldn't confidently assert that corporal punishment is a necessary feature of scholastic discipline, any more than I would assert that it is necessary to retain capital punishment in order to protect society from the murderer. But I do suggest that, if such punishments, whether in the world of school or in the wider sphere of law-enforcement, are indeed a necessary means, or even the most effective means, of maintaining order, then the authorities are betraying their trust if they refrain from imposing them simply because they cannot bear to contemplate the infliction of pain and suffering that their imposition would involve. They ought not to spare the rod simply in order to spare themselves.

Perhaps I have dwelt too long on capital and corporal punishment. They are the issues in regard to which the humanitarian tendency that I am concerned with shows itself most obviously. But that tendency is at work also, I think, on a wider front. It isn't merely the infliction of pain or suffering that is in question: it is the imposition of authority by force. There is observable today a strong anti-authoritarian tendency, a tendency that makes itself felt, especially, but not exclusively, among the younger generation. I don't think that it offers a real threat to society, at any rate in Britain. Most people, after all, accept the fact that the running of the country, the continuance of civil society, depends in the end upon force, and are prepared themselves to appeal to force in order to maintain it: if occasion arises, they will call the police. But there certainly is in Britain, as I imagine there is over here, an increasing number of people who won't go along with that at all. They are hostile to the concept of authority, and they regard the police as their natural enemies. Of course, the considerations that sway them are mixed, and often muddled. Some of them simply won't accept the fact that force should play a part in human affairs, in human relationships: that is the pure humanitarian attitude. Others resent the fact that force should be used in order to maintain a society that they disapprove of—a society that they disapprove of on egalitarian and libertarian grounds. That is a sort of political humanitarianism.

I said that I supposed that this anti-authoritarian attitude was observable over here. Since I first drafted this paper, I came upon an article that offers, in an entirely different context, some confirmation for this view. The editor of a magazine called the *Washington Monthly*, Mr. Tom Bethell, in reviewing some of the latest contributions to the literature concerning the Kennedy assassination, asks how it is that so many wild and monstrous theories of conspiracy are put forward, seeking to implicate in the assassination members of the Government, members of the Supreme Court, even the White House itself. "Why has this tendency become so noticeable recently?" asks Mr. Bethell. "At first, superficially, it may appear to be nothing more than a desire to avoid seeming naive, but there is more to it than this. It is more than a fear of seeming naive, there is an actual hostility, a burning rage, a desire to take the offensive against the *status quo* no matter what. Even a willingness, if necessary, to chop off the branch one is resting on. One is finally forced to the conclusion that there are in any society a good many individuals who naturally have or mysteriously develop a strong anti-authoritarian bias, a bias against any order, any institution, any stability, any society."

We have in Britain, as you have here, an increasing number of people who are hostile to authority; with us, they are a comparatively new phenomenon, and there aren't very many of them. Who are they? Where do they come from? What do they represent? What is it that they complain about? What is it that they want?

They would not claim to represent the oppressed and downtrodden, the underpaid and overworked, the poor, the lower classes. They come themselves, most of them, from bourgeois homes, and are inclined to be ashamed of the fact. They don't want to rebel, to organize revolt or revolution, to take over power from its present holders (though they are often duped and exploited by political manipulators of the extreme Left who wish to do exactly that). They are repelled by society as it is organized today, and feel that they have no place in it; it is dehumanized, dominated by money and machines, a world of pylons and nylons, of computers and commuters, ruled by forces, whether of the Right or the Left, over which the individual has no control—the individual, who is so occupied with the business of making a living that he is unable to live his own life. "Make love, not war!" is one of their messages to the world; "Make love, not money!" should surely be another.

People who recoil from the horrors of contemporary civilization—and I would be the last to deny the reality of those horrors—and who no longer accept traditional religious beliefs and the conventional code of morals, are all too likely to succumb to the appeal of a humanitarian gospel—Christianity without dogma or discipline: resist the police by offering them flowers, the emblem of love; overcome evil with good; love your enemies; love everyone, with an amorphous, all-embracing love —the sort of religion that inspires a community of hippies. In the words of a contemporary evangelist, "They bring the oldest message of love and peace and laughter, and trust in God and don't worry, trust in the future and don't fight; and trust in your kids, and don't worry because it's all beautiful and right."

I am against the hippies' ideal for two reasons.

First because I think that their muddled mysticism, their refusal to think and to be guided by reason, makes them an easy prey, not only to crackpots like Dr. Timothy Leary, from whom I have just been quoting, but to more mischievous rabble-rousers like Professor Herbert Marcuse, who seek to upset the foundations of society. Marcuse calls upon his young nonconformist followers to effect what he describes as "a methodical desublimation of traditional culture by means of counter-violence, direct action, and uncivil disobedience in every sphere of life." This social sabotage is to be directed against the beautiful in the established culture, against its all too sublimated, segregated, orderly, harmonizing forms. So he is all in favor of anti-art (pending the complete abolition of art by its absorption into life), together with black music and "its avant-gardistic white equivalent," and he approves of drug-taking (the trip, he says, involves the dissolution of the ego shaped by the established society) and of the atmosphere in which, as he puts it, "the hatred of the young bursts into laughter and song, mixing the barricade and the dance floor, love play and heroism [*heroism* is the reading of the Penguin text: I suspect a misprint for *heroin*]." He recommends the methodical use of obscenities, as practiced by black and white radicals, in order to effect "a methodical subversion of the linguistic universe of the establishment"; President X and

Governor Y he says, should be called Pig X and Pig Y, and addressed as mother-fuckers, because they are men who have perpetrated the unspeakable Oedipal crime. He approves not only of dirty language, but of dirty bodies, welcoming what he calls "the erotic belligerency in the songs of protest, the sensuousness of long hair, of the body unsoiled by plastic cleanliness."

That is humanitarianism gone wrong: violence called upon in aid of, in the name of, non-violence, with the promise of perpetual revolution.

There is a danger that those who are disenchanted with society as it is, and who have renounced the guidance of traditional wisdom, may fall victims to such desperate and dangerous nonsense.

My second reason for opposing the ideal lived out in a community of hippies—loving everyone, hating no one, harming no one, just co-existing peaceably—is that I think that this ideal, even if it could be achieved for society as a whole without revolution, is an evil one, and one that involves the sacrifice of everything that makes life worth living, everything that raises man above the level of domesticated animals.

The humanitarian ideal has, I know—in England at least—a special appeal to the young: I described earlier the life-style of the Oxford student—or of a large proportion of Oxford students—which is evidently inspired by a desire to return to nature, to recover the primitive innocence of man: the shaggy heads, the grotesque whiskers, the pathetic beards, the bare feet, the walking hand in hand, the patched clothes, the scruffiness, the dirt—all these are symbolic: they are the outward signs of a deep-seated desire to escape from the world as it is today into a primeval paradise. I don't think—I hope I'm not being too optimistic—that there is any likelihood of an increase in the hippy population in Great Britain, still less of their ideal winning general acceptance, though it is certainly not without influence on educated opinion. Most of the young over there learn to come to terms with the world in which they live, to make the best of it. Most of them, when they go down from the university, cut their hair, put on decent clothes, apply for jobs, and settle down to earn their livings: they enter the world instead of dropping out of it. Far be it from me to adopt a superior or patronizing attitude towards them, to say to them, when they join the ranks of the conformists, "I told you so." What I do want to say to them is that they should not regret the loss of their humanitarian ideals, and that they needn't feel ashamed of their apostasy.

Humanity, humaneness, is a good thing: it distinguishes men from animals, and civilized men from savages; but it is a good thing of which it is possible to have too much. Refusal ever to impose force on

57

others would mean the dissolution of civilized society. So long as there are bad men about, society relies ultimately upon force to restrain them: civilization depends upon the use of force just as much as it depends upon eliminating the abuse of force—indeed, it relies upon a proper use of force to protect its members from the wrongful use of force. You may recall the story of the shipwrecked sailors, who after tossing about for many days and nights in an open boat on uncharted seas, caught sight at last of an island. As dawn came on and they scanned the coast they were approaching, they perceived something—was it a tree?—standing upon the horizon. As they drew near, they made out what it was: a gibbet, with a dead body hanging from it. "Thank God!" exclaimed one of them, "it's a civilized country!" Well, I know what he had in mind: in a country where you may be executed by the hangman, at least you aren't likely to be scalped by savages or eaten by cannibals.

If a society refuses to contemplate the deliberate infliction of suffering upon its members, or by some of its members upon others, then it is at the mercy of its enemies, external or internal. The subsistence of law and order is the first essential of civilization.

Suppose a society from which, by a miracle, all wrong-thinking people were excluded, a community of gentle human beings, ruled by universal benevolence. Surely such a world would be the dreariest of deserts—no strife, yes, and no hate: but no excellence, no culture, no genius, no art, and no passionate love.

In the actual world, no extreme of excellence or virtue in human beings is conceivable without at least the possibility of its opposite—no passionate love without the possibility of hate, no ecstasy of pleasure without the possibility of pain. It is only in heaven that that condition will be transcended. Meanwhile, a wise man will make the best he can of this imperfect world. In a welter of good and evil, he will lead a measured life, compromising, yielding, standing firm, fighting if need be, keeping a clear head well screwed on, and a warm heart in the right place. In their eagerness to eliminate the evil, the humanitarians are ready to forgo the good; and their longing—did they but know it—is for the dead level of an impossible Utopia, devoid alike of pain, of passion, and of nobility.

A Utopia, indeed: but we need not look far to see something like such a community in action—or in passivity. In the aftermath of a pop festival, when the influence of the hysterical music has abated, or at a love-in, where the air is sweet with cannabis, one may observe the passionless population of a Woodstock world anticipating that Utopian bliss:

tender human creatures, tame and same, with the tameness and sameness of a herd of deer, or a school of porpoises, or a gathering of Galapagos lizards—a huddle of bodies snuggling, not struggling, on the smooth firm sand and gently respiring under the warm rays of the broad bland sun.

# Liberty

I suppose that almost everybody in Great Britain today, and almost everybody in the United States, if challenged on the subject of free speech, would say that he was in favor of it—though he might not be clear in his mind about what he meant by "free" or about what was to be included in the notion of "speech." Does "speech" in this context extend, for example, to printed and published words? Does it cover not only verbal but also pictorial and other forms of self-expression? Does it include every form of verbal utterance? In the course of arguments about free speech, extreme libertarians sometimes invoke the saying attributed to Voltaire: "I detest what you say; I will defend to the death your right to say it," as if Voltaire were asserting that everyone ought always to be allowed to say whatever he liked. But what the great freethinker was really contending for was (surely?) no more than the right to the uninhibited expression of opinion, the freedom of trade in ideas; he wasn't thinking about foul language, or obscenities. And it is the free expression of opinion that most people, I think, are concerned about when they say they are in favor of free speech.

In the United States freedom of speech is positively guaranteed by the constitution. Just what that freedom comprises has been laid down in a number of enactments and judicial decisions that constitute a whole branch of the law; and the same, making allowance for the fact that the English have no written constitution, is true in Great Britain. I am not concerned here with what the law actually is, either in Britain or in the United States. I am going to ask what the law ought to be, in regard to one particular area of human life or human conduct: how far ought the law to allow people freedom not merely to express opinions, but to express themselves? I think I detect, in society today, a strong feeling that human beings ought to be guaranteed by law not merely the right to express their opinions freely, but the right to express themselves as they choose, whether as creative artists or writers or in their everyday relations with each other. I should like to suggest that there is a danger that that claim may be pushed too far. Freedom to express one's self is a good thing, but it is a good thing that one can have too much of.

Most of the people who say simply that they are in favor of free speech would probably agree that there must be some limitations upon the freedom they contend for. For instance, everyone, except a professed anarchist, would surely agree that limitations may—indeed, should—be imposed by the civil law upon each citizen's right of free speech in order to protect the private rights of other citizens: the law of slander, the law of libel, and the law of copyright, all of them restrict—and, most people would say, very properly restrict—in the interests of other individuals, the fundamental right of every individual to say or print whatever he pleases. Restrictions upon this right are also imposed, in the interests of the public at large, by the criminal law. The law, at least the law of Britain, and I suspect the same is true in the United States, makes it a criminal offense to utter or to publish words likely to create a breach of the peace; and, in the field of security, the law makes it a criminal offense to publish in time of peace official secrets or seditious matter, and in time of war information that is likely to be of assistance to the enemy.

A recent example of encroachment by the criminal law in Britain upon this fundamental freedom is the Race Relations Act passed in 1965. This Act made it an offense to publish or distribute, with intent to stir up hatred against certain sections of the public specified in the Act, written matter which is insulting and likely to stir up such hatred. To constitute an offense it is not necessary, as it is under the Public Order Act, that the publication or distribution should be in a public place, or that it should be likely to cause a breach of the peace.

Most people would agree that all these restrictions upon the fundamental right to speak freely are justifiable on the ground that they help to preserve an orderly and civilized society; and until recently, I think, most people agreed that the law should aim also at preserving public decency, and that, with that end in view, it might impose restrictions not only on behavior, but also on speech and writing: if the law could properly forbid people to do in public things which offend other people's sense of decency, why shouldn't it forbid people publicly to say things—or exhibit things in writing, or for that matter in pictures—that give similar offense? In other words, it was generally accepted that the fundamental right of free speech and free expression is a right that is subject to the requirements of public decency just as it is subject to the requirements of public safety and public order.

This generally accepted position is now under attack from several quarters, both as regards speech and as regards other forms of self-expression. On what do the critics or attackers base their attack? To what arguments or principles do they appeal? There are, I think, three main grounds of objection.

First, the critics say that the concepts of obscenity and indecency are not constant, that they vary from place to place and age to age. What is considered indecent or obscene in one part of the world is perfectly acceptable in another; things that shocked our grandfathers, or even our fathers, seem quite innocuous to us today. To legislate against the obscene is like trying to legislate against a chameleon by reference to its color.

Further, say the critics, the concepts obscenity and indecency vary not only from one age and one place to another; there is rarely, if ever, agreement about them even in the same place and time; certainly there is not agreement in Great Britain today about what is obscene or indecent and what is not. Since the concepts are so uncertain in their denotation, it is impossible to frame a satisfactory law to deal with them; for it is a fundamental juridical principle that all laws, especially those to which a criminal sanction is attached, should state clearly and precisely what it is that they forbid.

Finally, the critics' third objection is that it isn't merely that no two people agree—or at any rate most people disagree—about the application of these concepts; the fact is (they say) that no one, no single person, can say what he himself means by them. When a man says "That's indecent," or "That's obscene," he is not indicating an attribute of the thing he refers to, but simply expressing his own reaction to it. To legislate against obscenity, therefore, is not only to legislate against a chameleon, it is to legislate against a chimera, a subjective fantasy.

To each of these three objections I think a satisfactory answer can be given.

The answer to the first objection is very simple. It is perfectly true that the things or the conduct thought or felt to be indecent or obscene differ widely in different countries, different societies, different civilizations, and they very also from one age, one generation even, to another. But, after all, each society legislates only for itself, and not for other societies, and only for its contemporaries and not for past or future generations. Therefore, provided the law takes account of the opinions and feelings prevailing in the community, and is so drafted that it can be adapted as those feelings and opinions change, it does not seem relevant to observe that it would have been inappropriate, or even absurd, to have passed such a law in a society where different feelings prevailed.

That is, I think, an obvious and sufficient answer; but one shouldn't dismiss this objector out of hand—his objection may conceal a deeper and more serious criticism. "I will tell you," he may really be saying, "why the notions of indecency and obscenity are so variable. It is because they are not founded upon reason, they are elements in a structure of conventions built out of, and upon, irrational taboos. Social progress consists in discarding taboos in favor of a rational structure of social rules; any law that bolsters up such conventions is an obstacle to progress." I think this criticism is ill-founded. I would question the premise that progress consists in, or depends upon, the discarding of non-rational conventions and taboos; and here, I suspect, I would have the support of social anthropologists, who would surely tell us that civilization is a highly artificial construction, and that to maintain it we must observe conventions which are in part rational and in part non-rational, and that it is impossible, and would be harmful even if it were not impossible, to eliminate the non-rational elements from the complex web of existing social convention. A society of human beings whose actions are governed entirely by rational considerations is hardly a conceivable, let alone an attainable, ideal. Indeed, it is not even a desirable ideal, for it is not true that the nearer we come to achieving it, the better life will be. We ought rather to aim at an appropriate blending of the non-rational and the rational: progress consists in the refinement, not in the elimination, of taboos; society, in short, should have the courage of its conventions.

So much for the objection based upon variability and irrationality.

The second objector is more practical in his outlook than the first. "Never mind," he says, "about other countries and other times; forget all *a priori* objections, based on irrationality and the like; let us assume that we want to legislate against obscenity in this country today. Very well: but how can we frame a satisfactory law? Even if we agree about the concepts of indecency and obscenity in the abstract, there is no agreement, when you come to apply them in practice, about what the things are that they denote: the concepts turn out to be hope-lessly vague and ragged at the edges. The writer, the artist, the publisher, the man in the street, all of them, if they are to be made liable to crim-inal prosecution, are entitled to be told in clear, precise, and definite terms what it is that they may not write or publish or say or do. It is impos-sible to frame a law against indecency that satisfies this requirement."

"Clear, precise, and definite terms"—the require-ment may seem very reasonable, but it is not quite as simple as it sounds. Clarity, precision, and definiteness are no doubt aims that every legislator sets himself, but it is not always possible for him to achieve them. Clarity is one thing, precision and definiteness (which we may call synonymous, I think, in this context) are another. Sometimes in a law both are attainable; sometimes precision but not clarity; sometimes clarity but not precision—it all depends upon the subject matter of the legisla-tion. The liability imposed by taxation, for in-stance, is always precise and definite, but the mean-ing of the law imposing it, as anyone will know who has had to deal with his own income tax, is not always clear; it is often exceedingly—and inevi-tably—obscure, because the cases that a taxing statute has to deal with are so intricate that they can only be provided for in very complicated and difficult terms. On the other hand, there are large areas in which, owing to the nature of the subject matter, the legislature cannot make rules as exact and precise as those that impose our tax liabilities; it has to forgo definiteness and to lay down a rule couched in clear but general terms, leaving it to a jury (with a judge's guidance) to determine whether in the circumstances of the particular case the defendant's conduct did or did not transgress the rule laid down.

Take the British Road Traffic Acts. They, or regulations made under them, lay down precisely the speed limit to be observed on certain roads and in certain areas; it is a question of fact, the answer to which is ascertainable by reference to a stopwatch, whether or not at any moment a driver is exceeding the relevant limit. He always knows, therefore, or can find out by looking at his speedometer, whether he is breaking the law or not. True enough: but motorists often, without exceeding the speed limit, drive recklessly or dangerously. Obviously, it is impossible to define recklessness in a statute, or to lay down precisely what shall constitute dangerous driving. The law does not on that account abandon the attempt to legislate against such driving; it simply prohibits dangerous driving, undefined, and leaves it to the jury in each case to say, in the light of the evidence, whether the defendant did or did not drive dangerously.

So, too, with cruelty to children: cruelty cannot

be defined in a statute so precisely that a man can say to himself "The Cruelty to Children Act is clear, precise, and definite: I can hit my child so many blows, of so much force, without transgressing the law; it is only if I exceed the cruelty limit clearly and precisely laid down by Parliament, that I shall be guilty." The legislature does not therefore say—and no one would wish it to say—"Since cruelty cannot be precisely defined, we will not prohibit it, but will leave it to the good feeling and self-restraint of the public, and of parents in particular, to see to it that children are not subjected to cruel treatment." No: the law prohibits cruelty, and leaves it to a jury of ordinary men and women to say whether in the given case the defendant's conduct is to be considered cruel.

In order to reach a verdict in such cases, a juryman must not have regard to what he himself would tolerate or disapprove, he must not ask himself what he would have done in the circumstances; he must put aside any peculiarities or prejudices of his own and decide, as best he can, what a reasonable person would do, or would tolerate, or would disapprove, in such a case. No doubt it is often difficult to ascertain this standard; and no doubt it is more often difficult to do so when you are dealing with indecency than it is in other areas—the borderline cases may be more numerous, partly because the borderline is in that area a shifting one

—but the task that confronts the jury is essentially the same. It is important to insist on this, because the critics of anti-indecency legislation often suggest that it imposes on juries an impossible task, and one that they do not have to carry out in cases arising out of legislation in other fields.

The fact, then, is that obscenity and indecency, like cruelty, negligence, and recklessness, are concepts that do not lend themselves to precise definition; but it does not follow from this that we should abandon the attempt to legislate against them.

The case presented by the third objector is the most plausible of the three, but it is no better founded than that of the other two. This objector does not concern himself with taboos and conventions, or with the fact that people often disagree about what is indecent and what is not; he takes a slightly different stand: "What you are complaining about," he says, "is nothing more than a personal reaction, and one which you cannot justify or even explain. You say you are shocked. What do you mean by 'shocked'? Weren't you shocked by newspaper reports of what went on in Vietnam? You say you are disgusted. Aren't you disgusted by what you read about the conditions in which the poor are housed in London slums? You complain about obscenities in the field of sex: is anything in the whole field of sex as obscene as apartheid in South Africa? You do not press for legislation against reports containing accounts of shocking, disgusting, obscenities like these. Even in the field of sex you betray the same inconsistency. A picture shocks you more than a verbal description of the thing depicted. You are not shocked by the idea of copulation in the marriage bed, but you are shocked by the idea of copulation in the street. What exactly is it that you are shocked by, and why is it that you are shocked by it? Perhaps it would do you good," he might add, with a touch of self-righteous asperity, "to be exposed to being shocked a bit more often, and then you might stop being shocked by things that in themselves are perfectly innocuous."

To this the complainant might well modestly reply: "Of course I know that all these words— "shocking" and "horrifying," "disgusting" and "obscene"—are sometimes applied to things quite different from the things I am complaining about. We may say, no doubt, that we are horrified by the news of a railway accident involving heavy loss of life, and that we are shocked when we hear that the Bishop has been murdered on the steps of the Cathedral; we are disgusted by the Government's measures to deal with unemployment, and if we want to convey to a friend our impression of the unpardonable ugliness of a third party, we may, perhaps, apply the word 'obscene' to his or her appearance. The feelings that I am talking about," he might go on to say, "which are experienced by most people with any refinement of sensibility, are quite different from the feelings at work in those examples. I cannot give you a clear and rational account of these feelings of mine, or enumerate the things that evoke them; they differ from indignation and moral disapproval, though they are sometimes accompanied by those emotions. My horror and disgust at actually witnessing an act of physical cruelty, for instance, are distinct from my pity for the victim and my moral disapproval of the act. Shame and disgust are usually evoked by functions of the body—for example, sexual intercourse, excretion, and parturition. These processes seem to be usually associated somehow with shame—the shame that craves privacy, the shame that Adam and Eve felt when they knew that they were naked. These feelings of shame and disgust are evoked—I don't know why—more easily by seeing something than by reading about it, unless the description is visually vivid. They are complex: the emotion felt is often accompanied by a physical reaction —a revulsion stronger than distaste and amounting sometimes to nausea. I know," he might conclude, "that these feelings—which I share, you must remember, with many people of normal sensibility, who are upset in the same way and by the same kinds of thing as I am myself—are not rational, and I know that they are difficult, perhaps just because they are not rational, to account for and to classify. But that does not make them any the less genuine, or any the less disagreeable, or any the less deserving—surely?—of the attention of the law."

That seems to me a more than sufficient answer to the third objection. Let me support it by an illustration. Suppose that a man, in full view and hearing of persons passing by him in the street, exposes his private parts, proceeds, for good measure, to masturbate in public, and, having masturbated, to utter a string of "four-letter" words, and to display a poster with filthy words and pictures printed on it. Surely it is as reasonable that the law should protect the passers-by from the third kind of affront (the filthy posters) as from the second (the foul language), and from the second as from the first (the indecent exposure), and surely it is as reasonable that it should protect passers-by from any one of these things as it is that it should protect them from actual physical assult? A law that in such a context protects the citizen's person but not his susceptibilities is like a divorce law that recognizes physical but not mental cruelty. And the fact that the complainant, where it is his susceptibilities that are assaulted, cannot define the kind of things that distress him, or explain why it is that they distress him as they do, affords no reason why the law should not protect him, so far as it can, from being subjected to the distress.

I should therefore look with favor on the idea of passing a law the aim of which was to protect the sensibilities of ordinary people from being outraged by the impact of things generally felt by them to be indecent. Of course, the law should not prudishly take account of mild or minor improprieties: whatever its wording, the test should be, in effect, whether the indecent act or thing complained of would be found outrageously offensive by a person of ordinary sensibility. It would be for the court, or jury, to decide in each case whether the limit had been exceeded.

I have spoken of protecting the public, and the examples I have given consisted of acts done in public places. Should the proposed prohibition apply only to things done or things exhibited in public? Many people who are in general opposed to censorship would, I believe, none the less approve of a law such as I have suggested, provided its scope was limited to acts publicly performed, or things publicly exhibited. And conversely, many people who strongly support a law forbidding indecency in public would hold that the line should be drawn there. If I may borrow the terminology of Roman law, they have no objection to the activities of the aedile, whose job it was to preserve decency on the streets; the man they object to is the censor, who claims jurisdiction over art and literature—books, pictures, the theater, and films. They would not mind a law that protected the passer-by from having indecencies actually obtruded upon him in public, but further than that they would not go.

They would say, presumably, that it should not be an offense just to publish indecent writings or drawings (or books containing them), or to offer them, whether gratis or for sale, to individual members of the public or, indeed, to the public at large; in their view, you should be liable to prosecution only if you actually exhibit them, or the indecent elements in them, in a public place. The bookseller may offer such books for sale in his shop, but he must not display them, open at an indecent passage or illustration, in his window where they may catch the eye of the innocent passer-by. So too with indecent theatrical performances and indecent shows (of films, pictures, and the like); provided these don't take place actually in public, no offense, they would say, should be deemed to have been committed, even if members of the public are allowed, or even invited, to view them, whether gratis or on payment of an entrance fee. In such cases, the argument would run, people can't complain that they have had indecency obtruded upon them; they needn't buy the book if it is offered for sale, or accept it if it is offered gratis; they needn't enter the premises where the performance is being given or the exhibition held. Once the aedile begins to turn the pages of a book, or crosses the threshold of premises that are private, he is exceeding his function as aedile and usurping the office of the censor.

I think that this contention takes too narrow a view of the legitimate functions of the aedile, and pushes too far the doctrine *caveat emptor* ("buyer's risk"); it fails to take account of the facts of life, of the way things actually happen. People when they buy a book don't always know, and can't be expected to know, what they will find inside it. Unless the law provides that a publisher must impress a special mark or label on all books likely to outrage generally accepted standards of indecency, and draw attention to indecent passages in otherwise innocent books by a note on the cover or the title-page—"outrageous indecencies on pp. 7, 26, 141–42, 210–15"—people won't know when they buy a book whether they are going to find indecencies inside it. To say that people who buy a book or a ticket of admission to a theater should have prepared themselves by reading what the critics in the weekly papers had to say about the book, and that if the critics have misled them about a play, they can always walk out of the theater, is not a realistic answer to the problem. No more is it realistic to say to people, if they complain about being confronted by an obscenity on television, "you can always switch the thing off." After all, many people watch television together with the family, and it is no use telling them to switch it off themselves if half the family want to keep it on. And where books are concerned, it is not only the purchaser that has to be considered: once a book is bought, it is liable to fall into the hands of all and sundry—and the person who picks it up and begins to read it unsuspectingly is, to all intents and purposes, in the same position as the innocent passer-by who finds himself confronted by an obscene picture on a billboard.

On the whole, therefore, I should be in favor of a law prohibiting the presentation of indecencies—I mean, indecencies that could properly be classified as outrageous—not only in public places, but also in books and magazines, and in plays, films, and exhibitions to which the public has access. If it is reasonable that the law should protect people from having thrust upon them, willy-nilly, things that outrage their sensibilities, it seems reasonable that it should likewise protect them from the risk of encountering such things at every turn in their daily life.

Some of the objections in principle that are advanced against legislation prohibiting indecency in books and plays and pictures are the same as those advanced against laws prohibiting indecency in public—the vagueness of the concept, the liability to change, the impossibility of defining it, and so on. I have already dealt with those objections; but there is a special objection that applies only to legislation in the field of art and literature, and to this I now turn.

The law, it is said, should not interfere in the field of books and plays and pictures, because Art should be above the law: it is monstrous, and it is absurd, to try to subject the creative activities of a painter or a writer, or an artist of any other kind, to the jurisdiction of a law court, giving to a judge or a jury the power of determining, when an artist's work is challenged, what subjects he may treat or depict and what language he may use in order to describe them. It would be equally monstrous, and even more absurd, to attempt to enforce decency by means of a list of prohibited subjects, words, and phrases, set out in a schedule to the relevant statute. Such absurdities, it is said, are the natural and inevitable result of transgressing the fundamental principle that the artist, working in his capacity as an artist, should not be subjected to the laws that regulate the activities of the ordinary citizen; the products of his creative gifts—in a word, Art—should be excluded from the scope of any law, or at least from the scope of any law intended to protect society from the impact of indecency. Of course, one can't help sympathizing with people who put forward a plea like that. Art is, indeed, in a sense, above and beyond the law: Acts of Parliament cannot control the artist's imagination;

Courts of Law cannot compel him positively to write or paint this rather than that; and where the State prevents him from publishing anything that is not acceptable to those in power (as it can do, and as it actually does in totalitarian countries) we feel that there is something not only wrong but shameful about the spectacle of "Art made tongue-tied by authority."

All this is true; but artists, none the less, live in the same world as ordinary men, and if they want to publish their work or to put it into general circulation they can't be exempted, simply on the ground that they are artists, from the laws that regulate society. When I say they can't be exempted, "can't," in this context, is literally true; for if the artist does claim exemption on that ground, he is confronted with an impossibility that is—as it were—built into his case. The law, he insists, must not be allowed to pronounce upon any alleged indecency in his work, because it is a work of art; the court must not be granted jurisdiction over him, because he is an artist. But what authority is to decide whether he and his work qualify for the claimed exemption? What but the law, operating by means of an Act of Parliament and administered by the courts? It is only by the law that anyone can be exempted from the law. The result of the artist's plea, therefore, if it were acceded to, would simply be to bring in the detested machinery at an earlier stage. And this would surely make matters worse, not better; for it must be even more intolerable for the artist that the law should decide the fundamental question whether he is an artist, than that it should decide the incidental question whether one of his works is outrageously indecent. But to say that the law may not pronounce upon his claim to the status of artist, and still to insist upon his right as an artist to exemption from censorial restrictions, is really to make the claim to be an artist a self-validating claim—if it is put forward it must be admitted—and to do this is tantamount to saying that in order to do justice to the claim of art there should, in the field of books and magazines and films and plays and pictures, be no restrictive legislation at all, or at any rate, none based on grounds of decency or morality.

Many of those who oppose censorship today would, of course, accept this conclusion—nor would they base their acceptance of it upon the view that the artist as such is entitled to any special privilege. Indeed, it is becoming rather old-fashioned nowadays to think of Art as a special kind of activity and to regard the artist as a special kind of person, entitled to extraordinary treatment. The line separating what is Art from what is not has worn as thin as the lines that used to separate one art from another: "We are all artists now"; and Art comprises every kind of happening or object, from the impersonal products of aleatory machines to the crudest results of uninhibited self-expression. Portraits of the artist's mother [*Mère de l'Artiste*] have gone out of fashion—a point nicely made by the organizers of a recent exhibition in Paris, which included an object, under a glass dome, labeled (correctly) *Merde de l'Artiste*—evidently a literal exemplification of the thesis that to produce a work of art the artist need do no more than just express himself.

The case, then, against censorial legislation in the field of books and pictures and plays and films must really be based, not upon high-flown appeals to the sacredness of Art or to the liberty of the individual, not upon *a priori* principles, but upon more pragmatic grounds. Society, it is said, loses more than it gains by the imposition of such laws; if you tell people who want to write or to paint or to produce a film or a play that they must not publish or exhibit anything that outrages contemporary sensibilities, you will deprive them of the freedom they need if they are to fulfill themselves as artists and give the world their best work: you don't only prevent them from publishing the indecent works at which the prohibitory law is aimed (which may themselves be supreme works of art, and which in a generation or so may be no longer thought to be indecent), but you cramp them, as it were, all round; an artist simply cannot work in fetters.

Therefore (the argument continues) the law should refrain from intruding upon the field of art and literature, not because the artist can claim a specially privileged position, but simply in the interests of society, which is enriched by the things that the artist produces and correspondingly impoverished if he is not allowed to produce them. On this view, in order to assure to creative writers the freedom that they need, we ought to put up with the unrestricted publication of indecent, obscene, and pornographic matter: whatever benefit may result from suppressing it, society will on balance, it is claimed, be a loser.

To adjudicate upon this claim, one would have to weigh the loss to the world of literature and art that would result from the prohibition of grossly indecent works against the damage that would be inflicted on society if no restriction were placed upon them. Under a system of censorship, literature perhaps would suffer: some writers and painters might feel inhibited, some masterpieces might remain unwritten, or might have to wait for publication (like Joyce's *Ulysses*) until prevailing standards changed. Against that one must set the suffering that would be inflicted upon individual sensibilities, and the damage that would be done to society at large, by removing all control over the publication of indecency, obscenity, and pornography. That damage is of two kinds. Over and above the outrage inflicted upon the sensibilities of ordinary people, to protect which should—I suggest—be the primary aim of censorial legislation, there is the positive influence for bad that the publication of indecent books and films may have upon those who read or see them. Since the possibility of such influence is often denied by opponents of censorship, I must explain carefully what I mean by it. I should have thought that it went without saying that we may be influenced—particularly when we are young, but also after we have grown up—by things we read or see; sometimes we are conscious of this influence, sometimes not; it operates, I should say, in varying degrees, sometimes for the better, sometimes for the worse. To be specific: it seems to me undeniable that, if we have read a book or poem or have seen a play or a film, our attitude to life may be altered by what we have read or seen—may be different from what it would have been if we had not read that book or poem, or seen that play or film. And what we read or see may affect not only our character but also our conduct: we may actually be impelled to go and do something that we saw enacted on the screen or read about in a book. The influence may be deep and lasting, or it may be trivial and temporary; it may be for the better, or it may be for the worse. A poem or a play may be either degrading or exalting in its effect; but that poems and plays do influence peoples' lives and conduct is, I should have thought, undeniable.

Of course, it is impossible to prove the truth of this proposition or to support it by precise statistics, either generally or in relation to a particular work. The same book or picture may leave some people unaffected, and may affect one person in one way, another in another; we can't say, therefore, that a particular film (for instance) will have a good or bad influence upon all the people who see it, or even upon an ascertainable proportion of them; nor can we say in advance that it will have a good or bad influence upon any particular person; nor, after a particular person has seen the film, can we gauge mathematically the extent of its influence upon him. And even if it does appear pretty plainly that a person was impelled to do something by (say) a film that he had seen—if, for instance (and this was a real case), a youth batters an old tramp to death or rapes a girl shortly after having seen a similar incident enacted in *A Clockwork Orange*—it is always possible to say that it was a coincidence: you can't prove that he wouldn't have battered the old tramp to death or raped the girl even if he hadn't seen the film. Even if he himself says, "It was seeing the film that made me do it," he may be self-deceived, or he may be seeking to transfer to others the responsibility for his act.

Now this general proposition, that things we read or see may influence us for better or worse, does not seem to me to be invalidated in the very least by our inability to offer a scientific proof of its truth, either generally or in relation to a particular work, or by our inability to support it by statistical evidence. To ask for scientific proof or statistical demonstration in such a case sounds, no doubt, impressive—it sounds as if the person asking for such proof was himself being scientific, when in fact his attitude and his approach are not scientific but the reverse: he is asking for a kind of proof, which, from the nature of the case, it is impossible to supply.

If one person is in love with another, his emotion will surely influence his attitude, his judgment, and his actions in relation to that person. It would be foolish (and, indeed, unscientific) to ask for a scientific definition of love or for a demonstration of the truth of the proposition that it influences people as I have suggested. And it would be wrong to say that the impossibility of providing such a demonstration and supporting it by statistical evidence shows that people are not really influenced in their relations with other people by their feelings for them.

Besides the direct influence of the unrestricted exhibition of indecent or obscene or sadistic art, we must consider also the indirect results. If one wants to get a fair idea of what those indirect results would be, one must take into account not only their impact upon those who actually read the books or see the films that contain them, but the effect that would be wrought upon people generally by the unrestricted publication and presentation of such things and the knowledge that their presentation and publication was permitted by law. In making one's estimate of that effect one has to rely on one's sense of how people's views are influenced, largely without their being aware of it, by what goes on around them, by the atmosphere of the society they live in.

I should say that the unrestricted circulation in the bookshops and on the bookstalls of grossly indecent and sadistic books and magazines, and the unrestricted presentation in theaters and cinemas of grossly indecent and sadistic films and live performances, coupled with the knowledge that these things were permitted by the law of the land, would make a difference to the way the general public regard the indecent and the inhumane, particularly in the field of sex and violence. People would unconsciously re-define these concepts, and alter their attitude towards the things they stand for: accepted standards of decency and humanity would themselves be modified; things that today disgust us by their indecency would no longer seem indecent, things that today horrify us by their brutality would no longer seem brutal, or not so shockingly brutal as they do now. The quality of life would in these respects undergo a gradual metamorphosis.

I say "a gradual metamorphosis," but I don't think that the process would be likely to be a slow one: people's attitudes and opinions on social questions nowadays change ever more swiftly, and nowhere more swiftly, it seems, than in this very field. If one wants to appreciate how rapid and how radical the change can be, one has only to switch on the television, or turn the pages of a newspaper, or visit a theater or a cinema. Things are described, language is used, scenes are depicted or enacted, that couldn't conceivably have found a place in print or on the screen or on the stage, twenty, ten, or even half-a-dozen years ago. There are for instance, films that shock the ordinarily sensitive person (though they may delight others) by their representation of cruelty or violence—films like *A Clockwork Orange*, or *Straw Dogs*, or *The Devils*, or *Beyond the Valley of the Dolls* (which was, in effect, a re-enactment of the killing of Sharon Tate and her friends by the fiend Charles Manson's pack of murderesses). Other films contain scenes of castration or coprophilia, or vivid presentations of sexual intercourse, normal or perverse; in Bertolucci's *Last Tango in Paris*, for instance, Marlon Brando, in full view of the audience, reaches for the butter and uses it as a lubricant, to facilitate an act that a few years ago, in the law-suit concerning *Lady Chatterley's Lover*, was deemed unmentionable.

I am not at the moment concerned with the question whether the change is for the better or the worse: I merely draw attention to the pace at which it is taking place. Here I should perhaps repeat that, though I believe that seeing obscenities in books or films may affect people's character and conduct, and will certainly affect people's attitude towards obscenity generally, this is not my primary reason for saying that their publication should be subject to control by law. What I propose is that the publication of obscenities should be prohibited in cases where it would transgress accepted standards of decency and humanity, and so outrage people's sensibilities; and it is the outrage upon people's sensibilities, not the effect it would have upon their characters or their behavior, that affords, in my opinion, the primary reason for holding that their publication should be restrained by the law.

I have posed the question whether the law should intervene in the field of indecency and obscenity, in art, in literature, in conduct; I have reviewed, very summarily, the arguments on either side; and I have outlined my reasons for holding that the law should so intervene.

I should like to conclude by touching upon a question that goes a little deeper—a question not so much for the lawyer as for the social anthropologist or the psychologist. The claim that the law should not intervene in the field of indecency is put forward, not of course by or on behalf of the decadent, the dissolute, the prurient, or the pornographers—though they may be its incidental and illegitimate beneficiaries. No: it is put forward by intellectuals and the *avant-garde*, to vindicate the right of the individual to express himself, to do his own thing without interference or inhibition. What is the impulse, the motive force, behind this individualistic pressure? It is a claim for a kind of liberty —the liberty to say what you like—for free speech. But it is in no sense political, though it is seized on and turned to their own purposes by social revolutionaries, like Professor Marcuse, who recommends the methodical use of obscenities as a revolutionary tool or weapon: to shock the Establishment is one way of shaking the Establishment. No: the pressure for liberty of self-expression is surely—like the egalitarian and humanitarian tendencies that were the subjects of my first two lectures—the expression of a mood of disenchantment with the social and economic order, of a desire to assert the claim of the individual in a world of combines and corporations, to vindicate the virtues of nature in the world of conventions and constraints, to do justice to those who wish, in a world of universal competition, not to surpass others, but simply to be themselves.

What I have been trying to do in these three lectures is to focus attention upon one or two points at which civilization itself seems to be threatened by contemporary tendencies—tendencies not in themselves deleterious, tendencies which if restrained within certain limits are actually civilizing tendencies, but which are dangerous if they are carried too far.

First, civilization depends upon the recognition and the cultivation of excellencies and superiorities; the maintenance of a civilized society, therefore, would be made impossible by a thorough-going egalitarianism. Competition in excellence is a civilizing force, and you do not discredit it by calling it a rat-race.

Second, civilization depends upon the maintenance of law and order, and law and order can't be maintained, in an imperfect world, without resort to force. Humanity, in the sense of humaneness, is not self-sustaining. You do not discredit force by calling it brute force.

Finally, civilized society exists for the individual —we can't remind ourselves of that too often in an age when the state has grown top heavy, and seems to crush all individual effort, all individual character, to leave us little room to fulfill ourselves: no wonder there exists today an almost desperate craving for self-expression. But society is pluralistic, and each individual must respect the individuality of his fellow citizens; he must exercise self-restraint, out of respect not only for the rights but for the feelings of his fellow men; self-expression is not self-validating, and affords no sovereign plea in its own defense when it collides with the common feelings and susceptibilities of mankind.

95    9   7 24

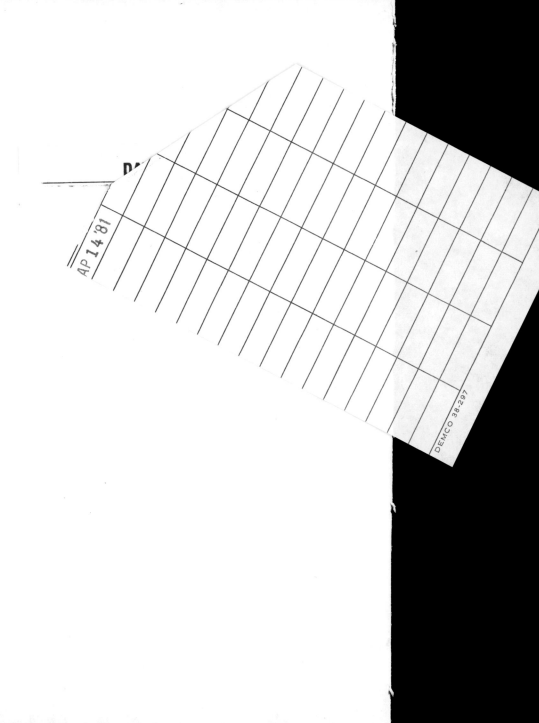

AP 14 81

DEMCO 38-297